25 Reproducible
Literature Circle
Role Sheets

for Fiction and Nonfiction Books

Written by Christine Boardman Moen

Illustrated by Dan Grossmann

Teaching & Learning Company

1204 Buchanan St., P.O. Box 10
Carthage, IL 62321-0010

This book belongs to

_____

DEDICATION

This book is lovingly dedicated to my sister Jane,
a lawyer even Shakespeare could have admired.

"The first thing we do, let's kill all the lawyers."
William Shakespeare, *Henry VI*

Cover by Dan Grossmann

Copyright © 1998, Teaching & Learning Company

ISBN No. 1-57310-141-9

Printing No. 98765432

Teaching & Learning Company
1204 Buchanan St., P.O. Box 10
Carthage, IL 62321-0010

Table of Contents

Dear Teacher or Parent,

I first learned about literature circles while attending a reading conference several years ago, and couldn't wait to get back to my classroom to try them out for myself! I wanted to use a student-centered learning strategy with a set of Newbery books that I had pulled together, and literature circles sounded exactly like what I wanted and what my students needed.

Like most things, we teachers try for the first time, I succeeded in many ways and failed in others, but I was so excited about literature circles and so determined to learn more about them that I called Dr. Harvey Daniels, who at the time was authoring *Literature Circles: Voice and Choice in the Student-Centered Classroom.* Dr. Daniels was wonderful as he explained that there was no one "right" way of doing literature circles. He recommended some basic guidelines and ended his conversation by saying, "Chris, don't stick to just the roles I've created. Create as many roles as you like." Well, I took Dr. Daniels at his word, and the results can be seen in this book.

Literature circles are student-centered book discussion groups. As the teacher observer, I've heard students share ideas, information and emotions they never would have with the old "teacher-asks-the-questions-students-give-the-answer" so-called "discussion" method. And literature circles utilize cooperative learning strategies. I've had classrooms of students with vast different reading abilities and attitudes learn to work together, help each other and enjoy reading and talking about books.

If you've never done literature circles in your classroom, please carefully read the introductory pages and then plunge in! It may not go perfectly the first time, but don't worry. You and your students will get better and enjoy yourselves more each time the circles meet.

And be prepared to be amazed and delighted by your students. Even though years have passed, I still remember a student Dialogue Designer's imaginary conversation between himself and Abraham Lincoln (*Across Five Aprils*) and the amazing drawing by a student of Bright Morning as she looked at her Womanhood Ceremony (*Sing Down the Moon*), Scene Setter.

I have so many other wonderful memories of my students and their literature circles, and we are creating even more memories as I continue to have literature circles in my classroom. In closing, I'd like to let some of my students speak for themselves about the rewarding experiences of participating in literature circles:

> "I especially liked the literature circles because there is no way that you can complete any of the roles without reading the book."   Katie

> "Another thing I learned (this quarter) was how to be in a literature circle. Even though I wasn't in the group I wanted, I learned to get along in not the best situation." Luke

> "I think the thing we have done this quarter that has benefited me the most (has been) the literature circles. I feel I have learned to be a better listener."   Carolyn

> "I like the literature circles the best out of the things I have learned (this quarter) because they are fun and (they) make it more fun to read books."   Joe

Happy, happy teaching!

Chris

Christine Boardman Moen

LITERATURE CIRCLE ROLE SHEETS

Literature circles and the roles that accompany this student-centered discussion strategy can be exciting additions to your literature-based classroom!

Literature circles are student book discussion groups in which each student has a role for which he or she is responsible.

The literature circle group meets at scheduled times while reading the book, and students rotate roles each time.

Advantages of Using Literature Circles in Your Classroom

Using literature circles in your literature-based classroom has many advantages over other book discussion methods. These advantages recognize that literature circles:

- **utilize cooperative learning strategies**

    Literature circles capitalize on the positive interdependence and individual accountability aspects that are hallmarks of cooperative learning. With literature circles, students work within a group setting with the common goal of sharing ideas about the same book. In order to achieve this common goal, students must fulfill the responsibilities of their individual literature circle roles.

- **allow all students to succeed regardless of reading level or ability**

    Student choice is important in literature circle book selection. First, students can choose from a teacher-selected *text set* of books which includes a variety of books of varying degrees of difficulty but ones which are based on the same theme, author or genre. At other times, students can create their own text sets. In both cases, students group themselves according to their interest in a certain theme, author or genre. Therefore, because groups are not permanent reading "ability groups," students move more easily between reading a variety of books of varying difficulty.

- **are student-centered and directed but are teacher facilitated**

    The teacher sets the parameters of the overall literature circle experience, but the students run the day-to-day operations. The teacher selects the end-date when all literature circles must be completed, but within that time framework, student groups decide the amount of pages to read, when to meet, and how the roles will rotate. The teachers can designate a text set and the roles from which students choose or students can designate a text set and a set of roles.

ADVANTAGES OF USING LITERATURE CIRCLES IN YOUR CLASSROOM

- **are organized around groups of students but allow for individual assessment**

  Authentic cooperative learning is based on group activities that allow students to be assessed as individual learners. Because students are observed as individuals working within a group, each can be given a participation grade based on a rubric. In addition, individual role sheets must be completed prior to the literature circle meeting. The role sheets are used to guide and promote group discussion; however, each student's role sheet should be turned in after the discussion so it can be graded individually. Finally, end-of-book projects can be used to assess individual student learning.

- **capitalize on how students personally respond to various types of literature**

  Each literature circle role sheet allows students to respond to the literature in a way only they can. Each role sheet allows students to respond to the literature using their own unique point of reference and prior knowledge. For example, four students reading the same book will respond differently in their individual groups even though each is performing in the role of Dialogue Designer.

LITERATURE CIRCLES DEFINED

Most often a literature circle is a group of three to five students gathered together to discuss the book they are reading or have just finished reading. Each has a role sheet he or she has completed prior to coming to the discussion, and each student uses the role sheet as a source for the group's discussion. Roles rotate within the group depending upon the length of the book and the grade level of the students involved. Older students reading longer books may meet four times while reading the book, whereas younger students may read a shorter book and meet only once or twice. The types of roles available to students and from which students choose are usually determined by the teacher. Some other general characteristics of literature circles include the following:

- students select their own book from the text set established by the teacher. (A text set is a group of different books related to a theme, author or genre. When selecting books for text sets, teachers often select books of varying lengths and reading levels to accommodate individual students' interests and abilities. Sample text sets with suggested roles appear later in this introduction.

- groups are formed according to book choice and exist only until the book has been read and the literature circle has met for the specified number of times.

- groups are given an end date and must decide how many pages to read in their book and how they will rotate their roles in order to meet the deadline.

- group members are given individual participation grades and are graded individually on their role sheets.

- role sheets serve as discussion starters since the purpose of literature circles is to encourage students to discuss the book. Roles can be somewhat artificial devices at first, but they quickly transform into discussion springboards as groups move to an integrated discussion of the book.

GETTING STARTED: ESTABLISHING TEXT SETS

Once you've decided to use literature circles in your classroom, the first thing to do is take an inventory of your classroom library and determine as many sources as possible for multiple copies of trade books. (A convenient set of inventory sheets can be found at the back of this book.) Having an inventory of books on hand and a list of sources for additional books are important time-savers because once students get into the swing of literature circles, they usually become voracious readers. Thus, your inventory sheets and list of sources will help you look for and organize books, books and more books!

Next, you must decide if you want to set up your circles based on genre, theme or author. Making this decision will probably hinge on the types of trade books available to you. Do you have a lot of historical fiction books, or can you get your hands on multiple copies of books that have survival as the main theme? Is your classroom filled with multiple copies of books by a specific author? You can always alternate your choice depending upon the availability of books for a text set and/or any special requirements of your curriculum. (A brief list of suggested text sets along with suggested role sheets appear later in this introduction.) A good rule of thumb is to have multiple copies of four different books for each text set. With this set up, Group A reads "A" book, Group B reads "B" book, Group C reads "C" book and Group D reads "D" book.

Once you've decided your text set, determine how many times you want each literature circle group to meet during the course of reading the book. Generally, literature circles meet for discussion after reading 25 to 30 pages. (The 25 to 30 pages is a general rule and students should read to the end of a chapter when necessary.) Students reading a book with 100 to 150 pages would meet three or four times to discuss the book. (Older students and more capable readers usually meet less frequently and read more pages.)

Since your text set consists of different books with varying numbers of pages, you must decide the number of times you want the circles to meet and allow the students, once they get into the circles for the first time, to determine the number of pages they must read prior to each circle meeting. For the sake of class organization, all literature circle groups usually end on the same date.

GETTING STARTED: GROUP MEMBERS AND ROLE SHEETS

The number of times the group will meet determines the number of group participants. If the circles will meet four times, then each circle should have four members so each member can assume a new role each time the circle meets. Although each circle reads a different book, all circles complete the same designated role sheets. (If you end up with an odd number, you can solve the problem in two ways: Add a fifth member to one or two groups and give that member a list of role sheets that do not rotate with the other group members, or drop one of the role sheets and create a three-member circle.) When possible, circles should not exceed five members nor have less than three members.

You've decided your text set, the number of times the circles will meet and the number of group members per circle. The next step is to determine the role sheets you will use with your text set. You have 25 different role sheets from which to choose, and almost any of them can be used with any genre, theme or author. So how do you decide which role sheets to use? To answer that question, you must think about the books in your text set. Do the stories in your text set have interesting vocabulary? Then include the Synonym Strip Maker role sheet. Are there authentic historical events and people woven into your historical fiction text set? Then you'll want to use the Time Liner and History Connector role sheets. Is the conflict in the stories of great interest and the scenes vividly described? If so, you'll want to include the Conflict Connector and the Scene Setter roles. The different combinations of roles are practically endless. Consequently, after examining each of the 25 role sheets from this book, select the roles you think will provide the most useful discussion prompts for your students. Remember: Each student will get to assume each of the roles you select because the roles rotate each time the circle meets.

After you've decided your role sheets, the next step is to give students a brief explanation of literature circles before giving a book talk and allowing students to choose their books. (A good way to introduce literature circles to first-time students is to explain the process by completing a **Literature Circle Overview** sheet with the class. Completing the sheet doesn't explain the discussion that takes place during a circle, but it does explain who does what and when. Once students understand how a circle is set up and how it runs, they can focus on understanding how the various role sheets can help them have good literature circle discussions.)

Your book talk can be anything from an elaborate presentation to reading a review of the book and passing the book around so the students can read the blurb on the back.

Some simple ideas include the following:

- show students the cover art and the title of the book and have them make predictions about what the book is about. Once they've made their predictions, read the blurb on the back of the book or inside cover to see how accurate their predictions were.

- read the first few pages of the book and ask students to make predictions about the story. Ask students to compare and contrast the story beginning with other books they've read.

- show students different books written by the same author. Ask those students who have read books by this author to tell the class what they liked about the books and the way the author wrote them. Introduce the text set book and read the book's author notes and blurb.

- gather cross-curriculum nonfiction books about a topic or issue that is dominant in the text set book. Have students break into pairs and find an interesting fact to share with the class. Introduce the text set book by relating some of the facts to the book. For example, if students are reading *Across Five Aprils*, relate the facts on the Civil War and Abraham Lincoln to the events in the book.

- read aloud the description of the book's main character and have students try to guess his or her name. After guessing, read the book's blurb and tell the students the character's name.

- play any musical pieces mentioned in the book or show any art selections mentioned in the book and explain how each is related to the story.

Once you've introduced the books to your class, students sign up immediately for their book choice. Students list their book choices in order of preference and turn their list into you. (Having students write out their choices immediately after your book talk discourages "cliques" and establishes the expectation that students will be working with a variety of students during literature circles.)

After you've received the students' book choices, determine each circle's group members. Not every student will get his or her first or even second choice. Keep a list of those students who do not get their first or second choice so they are able to get their choice next time you do literature circles with a new text set. Of course, even though students determine groups by book choice, you must do some of the grouping. Since grouping students is often more of an art than it is a science, it's usually–but not always–a good idea to have boy-girl groups and avoid groups that include students who are all too shy to talk or are all to talkative to listen.

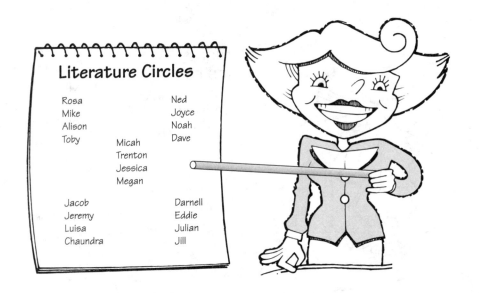

Getting Started: Modeling Role Sheets

You're almost ready to launch your circles! However, if it's the first time your students have participated in literature circles or if your class is comfortable with circles, but you've chosen roles they've never used before, it's important to model or "walk through" the role sheets and explain how a literature circle unfolds. (When students participate in literature circles the first few times, they tend to "cover" the material on each student's role sheet. However, by the time a literature circle meets for its third time, students are usually using the roles as prompts and discussion is enthusiastic, responsive and supported with examples and details taken directly from the book.)

The best way to model is to have students read the same short story or short nonfiction piece. Make copies of the role sheets as you want to introduce to the students and also make overhead transparencies of each of them. For the sake of illustration, let's assume that you've had your students read "The Three Little Pigs," and you've selected **Time Liner, Quotable Quotations Quizzer, Plot Person** and **Dialogue Designer** as roles. (The same modeling procedure would apply with a nonfiction piece of literature, although the roles would probably be different.)

To model these roles, you'd first distribute copies of the **Time Liner** role sheets to the students and put your transparency on the overhead. As a class, ask students to identify what they would consider the important events in the story. List these events on the board or another transparency. Next, ask students as a class to select which events to include on the time line. Students list these events correctly on their role sheets while you list them on your transparency.

Not by the hair of my chinny chin chin. I will not let you in!

To model the **Quotable Quotations Quizzer** role, follow the same procedure above asking students to identify significant quotations such as "I'll huff and I'll puff and I'll blow your house in!" and "Not by the hair of my chinny chin chin. I will not let you in!" Again, complete the overhead transparency role sheet as students complete their sheets.

To model the **Plot Person** role, explain that the **Plot Person** tells the plot of the story using the S: Somebody, W: Wanted, B: But, S: So method. (The completed plot chart for "The Three Little Pigs" appears on the **Plot Person** role sheet [page 32].) To get practice with the SWBS method, try using it with another fairy tale such as "Goldilocks and the Three Bears." Your completed chart may look something like this:

S: The three bears.

W: Wanted to go for a walk in the woods.

B: But while they were out, an intruder by the name of Goldilocks broke little bear's chair, ate his porridge and fell asleep in his bed.

S: So when they came home and discovered the intruder, their appearance frightened Goldilocks and she ran away.

Now complete the overhead transparency role sheet for "The Three Little Pigs" as students fill out their copies.

Finally, to model the **Dialogue Designer** role sheet, ask the students as a group to contribute their comments as they pretend they are the brother of the Big Bad Wolf who meets the Third Little Pig at a community picnic where the big event is the race between the tortoise and the hare. As students contribute, complete the transparency role sheet while students complete theirs.

GETTING STARTED: WRAP-UP

While the class has been working as a group to complete the role sheets, much of the discussion that's taken place is exactly the type of discussion that occurs in a literature circle. Point this out to the students by reviewing each of the role sheets and reminding students of some of the significant comments made during each role completion. It's important, however, that students understand that role sheets are completed **before** literature circles meet. As a result, discussion time is not spent on how a role sheet should be completed but rather circle time is spent discussing the information on the role sheet and how it relates to the information on other students' role sheets. Thus, each role prompts students to take a unique and personal look at the assigned reading and share that outlook with other students.

GETTING STARTED: READY, SET, GO!

You've gathered, planned, grouped and modeled, and now you're finally ready to go! Distribute the books, designate each circle's members and their classroom discussion area and hand out the **Literature Circle Overview** sheet for each group to complete. (Students may need help completing the sheet the first time. Consequently, it may be helpful to provide students with the completed sample overview sheet that appears on page 23.) The circles complete the overview sheets, which are posted in the classroom, and everyone gets to reading!

14

Books Used in Text Sets

Across Five Aprils, Irene Hunt, New York: Berkley Publishing Group, 1991.

Belle Prater's Boy, Ruth White, New York: Farrar, Straus & Giroux, Inc., 1995.

Behind the Blue & Gray: The Soldier's Life in the Civil War, Delia Ray, New York: Dutton Children's Books, 1991.

Beyond the Western Sea: Books One and Two, Avi, New York: Orchard Books, 1996.

The Boys' War, Jim Murphy, Boston: HarperCollins Children's Books, 1990.

Brian's Winter, Gary Paulsen, New York: Delacorte Press, 1996.

The Bridge to Terabithia, Katherine Paterson, New York: HarperCollins Children's Books, 1977.

Call It Courage, Armstrong Sperry, New York: Simon & Schuster Children's, 1968.

Dogsong, Gary Paulsen, New York: Simon & Schuster Children's, 1985.

Dragonwings, Laurence Yep, New York: HarperCollins Children's Books, 1977.

The Drummer Boy of Vicksburg, G. Clifton Wisler, New York: Lodestar Books, 1997.

The Flip-Flop Girl, Katherine Paterson, New York: Dutton Children's Books, 1994.

Gentle Annie: The True Story of a Civil War Nurse, Mary Francis Shura, New York: Scholastic Inc., 1994.

A Girl Named Disaster, Nancy Farmer, New York: Orchard Books, 1996.

The Great Fire, Jim Murphy, New York: Scholastic Inc., 1995.

The Great Gilly Hopkins, Katherine Paterson, New York: HarperCollins Children's Books, 1978.

Hatchet, Gary Paulsen, New York: Simon & Schuster Children's, 1987.

Hunting Neptune's Giants: True Stories of American Whaling, Catherine Gourley, Brookfield, CT: Millbrook Press, Inc., 1995.

Island of the Blue Dolphins, Scott O'Dell, New York: Yearling Books, 1987.

Jip: His Story, Katherine Paterson, New York: Lodestar Books, 1996.

Julie of the Wolves, Jean Craighead George, New York: HarperCollins Children's Books, 1972.

Kids at Work: Lewis Hine and the Crusade Against Child Labor, Russell Freedman, Boston: Houghton Mifflin Co., 1994.

Lincoln: A Photobiography, Russell Freedman, Boston: Houghton Mifflin Co., 1987.

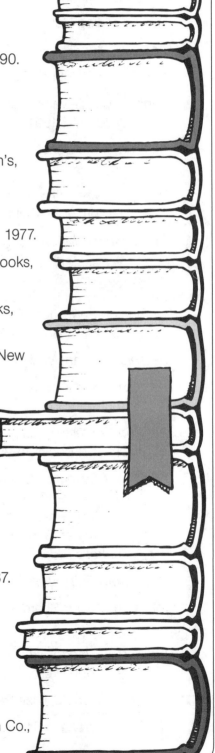

My Side of the Mountain, Jean Craighead George, New York: Dutton Children's Books, 1988.

A Nation Torn, Delia Ray, New York: Puffin, 1996.

Old Yeller, Fred Gipson, New York: HarperCollins Children's Books, 1990.

Once on This Island, Gloria Whelan, New York: HarperCollins Children's Books, 1995.

Rascal, Sterling North, New York: Avon, 1976.

The River, Gary Paulsen, New York: Doubleday & Co., Inc., 1991.

Safe Return, Catherine Dexter, Candlewick Press, 1996.

Shiloh, Phyllis Reynolds Naylor, New York: Simon & Schuster Children's, 1991.

The Sign of the Beaver, Elizabeth George Speare, New York: Dell Publishing Co., Inc., 1993.

The Sign of the Chrysanthemum, Katherine Paterson, New York: HarperCollins Children's Books, 1988.

Sing Down the Moon, Scott O'Dell, Boston: Houghton Mifflin Co., 1970.

Sounder, William H. Armstrong, New York: HarperCollins Children's Books, 1969.

The Talking Earth, Jean Craighead George, New York: HarperCollins Children's Books, 1983.

The Thief, Megan Whalen Turner, New York: Greenwillow Books, 1996.

The 13th Floor: A Ghost Story, Sid Fleischman, New York: Greenwillow Books, 1995.

The True Confessions of Charlotte Doyle, Avi, New York: Orchard Books, 1990.

The Tucket Adventures:
　　Call Me Francis Tucket, Gary Paulsen, New York: Delacorte Press, 1995.
　　Mr. Tucket, Gary Paulsen, New York: Delacorte Press, 1994.
　　Tucket's Ride, Gary Paulsen, New York: Delacorte Press, 1997.

A View from Saturday, E.L. Konigsburg, New York: Atheneum, 1996.

Walk Two Moons, Sharon Creech, New York: HarperCollins Children's Books, 1994.

The Watsons Go to Birmingham–1963, Christopher Paul Curtis, New York: Delacorte Press, 1995.

The Westing Game, Ellen Raskin, New York: Dutton Children's Books, 1978.

Where the Red Fern Grows, Wilson Rawls, New York: Bantam Books, Inc., 1984.

Suggested Text Sets and Role Sheets

Historical Fiction

Text Set

Island of the Blue Dolphins by Scott O'Dell

Safe Return by Catherine Dexter

Dragonwings by Laurence Yep

Beyond the Western Sea: Books One and Two by Avi

Suggested Roles

Culture-Customs Commentator

Story Tree Teller

Synonym Strip Maker

Passage Master

Text Set

Across Five Aprils by Irene Hunt

Once on This Island by Gloria Whelan

Sing Down the Moon by Scott O'Dell

The Drummer Boy of Vicksburg by G. Clifton Wisler

Suggested Roles

Time Liner

History Connector

Mapmaker

Character Sketcher

Nonfiction

Text Set

Hunting Neptune's Giants: True Stories of American Whaling by Catherine Gourley

Lincoln: A Photobiography by Russell Freedman

Kids at Work: Lewis Hine and the Crusade Against Child Labor by Russell Freedman

The Great Fire by Jim Murphy

Suggested Roles

Math Magician

Solutions Suggester

Fact Finder

Quotable Quotations Quizzer

MYSTERY/ADVENTURE

Text Set

The Westing Game by Ellen Raskin

The 13th Floor: A Ghost Story by Sid Fleischman

The Thief by Megan Whalen Turner

The True Confessions of Charlotte Doyle by Avi

Suggested Roles

Scene Setter

Recipe Reader

Decision Director

Plot Person

REALISTIC FICTION

Text Set

Hatchet by Gary Paulsen

The Talking Earth by Jean Craighead George

My Side of the Mountain by Jean Craighead George

A Girl Named Disaster by Nancy Farmer

Suggested Roles

Science-Geography Genius

Mapmaker

Dialogue Designer

Sequel-Prequel Person

Text Set

A View from Saturday by E.L. Konigsburg

Shiloh by Phyllis Reynolds Naylor

Walk Two Moons by Sharon Creech

The Watsons Go to Birmingham–1963 by Christopher Paul Curtis

Suggested Roles

Have-in-Common Connector

Tangrams Teller

Wordsmith

Character Sketcher

AUTHOR STUDY

Text Set: Books by Katherine Paterson

The Bridge to Terabithia

The Flip-Flop Girl

The Great Gilly Hopkins

Jip: His Story

The Sign of the Chrysanthemum

Suggested Roles

Character Sketcher

Author Authority

Plot Person

Conflict Connector

Passage Master

Text Set: Books by Gary Paulsen

Hatchet

The River

Dogsong

Brian's Winter

The Tucket Adventures (three books, see page 16)

Suggested Roles

Character Sketcher

Author Authority

Conflict Connector

Scene Setter

Wordsmith

TLC10141 Copyright © Teaching & Learning Company, Carthage, IL 62321-00

TEXT SETS BY THEME

THEME: GROWING UP AND BEING A MEMBER OF A FAMILY

Text Set

Sounder by William H. Armstrong

The Watsons Go to Birmingham–1963 by Christopher
   Paul Curtis

A View from Saturday by E.L. Konigsburg

Belle Prater's Boy by Ruth White

Suggested Roles

Character Sketcher

Passage Master

Have-in-Common Connector

Solutions Suggester

THEME: ANIMALS AS CENTRAL CHARACTER AND THE YOUNG PEOPLE WHO LOVE THEM

Text Set

Old Yeller by Fred Gipson

Rascal by Sterling North

Shiloh by Phyllis Reynolds Naylor

Where the Red Fern Grows by Wilson Rawls

Suggested Roles

Scene Setter

Plot Person

Dialogue Designer

Sequel-Prequel Person

Theme: Surviving the Elements and Learning About Ourselves

Text Set	**Suggested Roles**
Julie of the Wolves by Jean Craighead George	Science-Geography Genius
Call It Courage by Armstrong Sperry	Decision Director
Hatchet by Gary Paulsen	Wordsmith
The Sign of the Beaver by Elizabeth George Speare	Conflict Connector

Theme: Real People Enduring Civil War

Text Set	**Suggested Roles**
The Boys' War by Jim Murphy	Mapmaker
A Nation Torn by Delia Ray	Time Liner
Gentle Annie: The True Story of a Civil War Nurse by Mary Francis Shura	Synonym Strip Maker
Behind the Blue & Gray: The Soldier's Life in the Civil War by Delia Ray	Fact Finder

ROLE SHEET RECORD-KEEPER	Character Sketcher	Fact Finder	Synonym Strip Maker	Author Authority	Plot Person	History Connector	Scene Setter	Culture-Customs Commentator	Passage Master	Sequel-Prequel Person	Science-Geography Genius	Story Tree Teller	Dialogue Designer	Decision Director	Conflict Connector	Solutions Suggester	Recipe Reader	Have-in-Common Connector	Mapmaker	Progress-Process Person	Time Liner	Tangrams Teller	Quotable Quotations Quizzer	Math Magician	Wordsmith
...oss Five Aprils																									
...le Prater's Boy																									
...hind the Blue & Gray																									
...yond the Western Sea																									
...e Boys' War																									
...an's Winter																									
...e Bridge to Terabithia																									
...ll It Courage																									
...gsong																									
...agonwings																									
...e Drummer Boy																									
...e Flip-Flop Girl																									
...ntle Annie																									
...Girl Named Disaster																									
...e Great Fire																									
...e Great Gilly Hopkins																									
...tchet																									
...nting Neptune's Giants																									
...and of the Blue Dolphins																									
...: His Story																									
...lie of the Wolves																									
...ds at Work																									
...coln: A Photobiography																									
...Side of the Mountain																									
...Nation Torn																									
...d Yeller																									
...ce on This Island																									
...scal																									
...e River																									
...afe Return																									
...iloh																									
...e Sign of the Beaver																									
...e Sign of the . . .																									
...ng Down the Moon																									
...under																									
...e Talking Earth																									
...e Thief																									
...e 13th Floor																									
...e True Confessions . . .																									
...e Tucket Adventures																									
...View from Saturday																									
...alk Two Moons																									
...e Watsons Go to . . .																									
...e Westing Game																									
...here the Red Fern Grows																									

LITERATURE CIRCLE OVERVIEW

Names of literature circle group members

_____   _____

_____   _____

Title of book group is reading: _____

The group has decided to meet on the following dates and have the designated pages read:

Date: _____   Read from page _____ to _____

Date: _____   Read from page _____ to _____

Date: _____   Read from page _____ to _____

Date: _____   Read from page _____ to _____

The roles will rotate as follows:

Name/Role   Date: _____   Name/Role   Date: _____

1. _____   1. _____

2. _____   2. _____

3. _____   3. _____

4. _____   4. _____

Name/Role   Date: _____   Name/Role   Date: _____

1. _____   1. _____

2. _____   2. _____

3. _____   3. _____

4. _____   4. _____

SAMPLE

LITERATURE CIRCLE OVERVIEW

Names of literature circle group members

<u>Andrew Stayton</u>   <u>Maria Gonzales</u>

<u>Rosa Lopez</u>   <u>Nick Adams</u>

Title of book group is reading: <u>The Watsons Go to Birmingham—1963</u>

The group has decided to meet on the following dates and have the designated pages read:

Date: <u>Monday, February 3</u>   Read from page <u>1</u> to <u>46</u>

Date: <u>Thursday, February 6</u>   Read from page <u>47</u> to <u>99</u>

Date: <u>Monday, February 10</u>   Read from page <u>100</u> to <u>148</u>

Date: <u>Thursday, February 13</u>   Read from page <u>149</u> to <u>210</u>

The roles will rotate as follows:

Name/Role   Date: <u>Monday, February 3</u>

1. <u>Andrew</u>   <u>Have-in-Common Connector</u>

2. <u>Rosa</u>   <u>Tangrams Teller</u>

3. <u>Maria</u>   <u>Wordsmith</u>

4. <u>Nick</u>   <u>Character Sketcher</u>

Name/Role   Date: <u>Thursday, February 6</u>

1. <u>Andrew</u>   <u>Tangrams Teller</u>

2. <u>Rosa</u>   <u>Wordsmith</u>

3. <u>Maria</u>   <u>Character Sketcher</u>

4. <u>Nick</u>   <u>Have-in-Common Connector</u>

Name/Role   Date: <u>Monday, February 10</u>

1. <u>Andrew</u>   <u>Wordsmith</u>

2. <u>Rosa</u>   <u>Character Sketcher</u>

3. <u>Maria</u>   <u>Have-in-Common Connector</u>

4. <u>Nick</u>   <u>Tangrams Teller</u>

Name/Role   Date: <u>Thursday, February 13</u>

1. <u>Andrew</u>   <u>Character Sketcher</u>

2. <u>Rosa</u>   <u>Have-in-Common Connector</u>

3. <u>Maria</u>   <u>Tangrams Teller</u>

4. <u>Nick</u>   <u>Wordsmith</u>

MANAGEMENT, ASSESSMENT AND TROUBLESHOOTING

- When selecting books for text sets, choose books of varying lengths and reading levels to accommodate individual students' interests and abilities.

- Affix a copy of each group's completed **Literature Circle Overview** to a folder or large envelope. After each literature circle meets, collect its completed role sheets and put them in the folder or envelope for assessment.

- Assign a specific meeting place in the classroom for each literature circle group. The group is to meet in this assigned place each time it has a discussion.

- Carry a clipboard or folder onto which you've attached note cards for the purpose of recording anecdotal observations. Anecdotal records can be used to assign participation grades if you choose to use a grading system. **OR**

- Use the **Observation-Feedback Chart** on page 26 to assign participation grades. (Decide the best method of observation for you. You can observe each group once or as often as the group meets. You can even decide to be in two or three places at the same time by observing one group and simultaneously audiotaping other groups.)

- One day per week is designated as make up day, and all students who were absent the day their literature circle met, have a literature circle of their own with the teacher as the moderator. (Because the make up literature circle discussions end up being about all of the books, students often are left wanting to read more than their chosen book from the text set.) Groups missing more than two members should have their circle time rescheduled.

- Create a grading-assessment tool with which you are comfortable that balances the completion of the role sheets with the participation in literature circles.

- Students who are habitually unprepared and/or disruptive are removed from the literature circle and are required to complete teacher-assigned role sheets and projects. Students are never removed permanently from the literature circle experience–only for the remainder of the reading of the current book.

Resources for Literature Circles

Books

Children's Voices by Bernice E. Cullinan. IRA, 1993.

Literature Circles: Voice and Choice in the Student-Centered Classroom by Harvey Daniels.
  Highlights for Children, 1994.

Literature Circles and Response by Bonnie Campbell Hull (ed.) et al.
  Christopher-Gordon Publishers, 1995.

Teaching with Newbery Books by Christine Boardman Moen.
  Scholastic, 1995.

Magazines

Book Links

Book List

The Horn Book

Library Journal

The Reading Teacher (IRA)

School Library Journal

Libraries

Your local library, of course, is a great resource for books, book lists, review journals, etc. Don't overlook any nearby college libraries (or their websites) for themed lists of children's and young adult books.

Internet

www.ala.org/alsc/newbery.html (reviews of Newbery and Caldecott winners)

www.amazon.com ("Earth's Biggest Bookstore," lists of children's and young adult books)

www.acs.ucalgary.ca/~dk brown/index/html (The Children's Literature Web Guide)

www.bookwire.com/index/Childrens-Publishers.html (lists of publishers with links to websites)

OBSERVATION-FEEDBACK CHART

Date: _____ Book: _____ Pages: _____

This is the group's   1st   2nd   3rd   4th   literature circle on this book. (Circle one.)

Group members' names: 1. _____   2. _____

3. _____   4. _____   5. _____

Student numbers are used to indicate observations I made in your group today.

Positive Behaviors

a. _____ was thoroughly prepared with completed role sheet and had book with him or her during discussion.

b. _____ respected other people's opinions by asking for clarification or more information.

c. _____ encouraged others to speak and did not dominate the discussion.

d. _____ cited pages and used quotations to support conclusion(s).

e. _____ paraphrased either book content and/or other students' comments to help clarify discussion.

f. _____ hitchhiked or piggybacked on someone else's comments/quotations to further discussion.

g. _____ moved the discussion forward by resolving any differences of opinions or conflict of personalities.

h. _____ made connections between the different information supplied by the various roles.

Negative Behaviors

a. _____ did not have role sheets completely done and/or did not have book with him or her.

b. _____ gave opinion(s) but did not support conclusion(s) by quoting from the text.

c. _____ was disruptive and distracting with inappropriate comments/behavior.

d. _____ made no attempt or very limited attempt to discuss the assigned text with group.

One suggestion I have for improving your discussion: _____

_____

I especially liked: _____

_____

_____

CHARACTER SKETCHER

Your role as the Character Sketcher is to help your group members better understand the characters in your book. In addition, the Character Sketcher helps the group recognize any changes in personal growth in the characters as well as how the characters view each other. Characters reveal themselves by what they say and do and by what others say about them. Using these as guides, list characteristics on the left side of the page and examples from the book that support these characters traits on the right. Be sure to include pages numbers so your group can refer to them during discussion.

Character's Name _____

Characteristic	Supporting Example
1.	1.
2.	2.
3.	3.

Character's Name _____

Characteristic	Supporting Example
1.	1.
2.	2.
3.	3.

Character's Name _____

Characteristic	Supporting Example
1.	1.
2.	2.
3.	3.

Name _____

FACT FINDER

As the Fact Finder, it is your role to find interesting and important facts in your book to share with your literature circle discussion group. Your facts can include numbers.

↓ Tape or glue edges together. ↓

Front

Fact Card

Book Title: _____

Author: _____

Fact Topic: _____

Fact: _____

Back

Draw, diagram or chart your fact.

This Fact Card belongs to: _____

SYNONYM STRIP MAKER

The Synonym Strip Maker helps group members increase their vocabularies by creating a set of synonym strips and sharing them with the group. Your role is to select unfamiliar words from the story and create a synonym strip for each of the words.

As you read, use sticky notes to tag pages that contain unfamiliar words. After you've finished reading your assigned pages, go through the tagged pages and select words for your strips. Copy the sentences onto the strips below, making sure to include the page numbers and to underline the vocabulary word in each sentence. Cut each strip along the dotted lines, making sure you do not cut the strips apart. Next, use a thesaurus and select three synonyms for each new word and copy the synonyms onto the back of each strip. During your group discussion, have your group members take turns reading the sentences and substituting the synonyms for the vocabulary words.

Sentence 1: _____

_____ Page: _____

Sentence 2: _____

_____ Page: _____

Sentence 3: _____

_____ Page: _____

Sentence 4: _____

_____ Page: _____

Sentence 5: _____

_____ Page: _____

Sentence 6: _____

_____ Page: _____

SYNONYM STRIP MAKER

- -

Sentence 7: _____

_____ Page: _____

- -

Sentence 8: _____

_____ Page: _____

- -

Sentence 9: _____

_____ Page: _____

- -

Sentence 10: _____

_____ Page: _____

- -

Sentence 11: _____

_____ Page: _____

- -

Sentence 12: _____

_____ Page: _____

- -

Sentence 13: _____

_____ Page: _____

- -

Sentence 14: _____

_____ Page: _____

- -

AUTHOR AUTHORITY

The purpose of the Author Authority role is to help literature circle group members become more familiar with the author of the book the group is reading. In interviews, authors often talk about their various books and discuss where they got their ideas, the research they had to do in order to write their books and if anything in any of their books is autobiographical.

Numerous books, magazines and the jacket covers of books themselves will give information about authors. After researching the author of your book, try to supply the following information so you are able to share it with your group members.

Author's full name and pen name if applicable: _____

Author's country of origin and where author is currently living: _____

Other books this author has written: _____

_____

_____

Comments this author has made about books/writing: _____

_____

_____

Two interesting facts about this author: _____

_____

_____

Comments this author or others have made about the book you are reading: _____

_____

_____

Sources where you got your information: _____

_____

_____

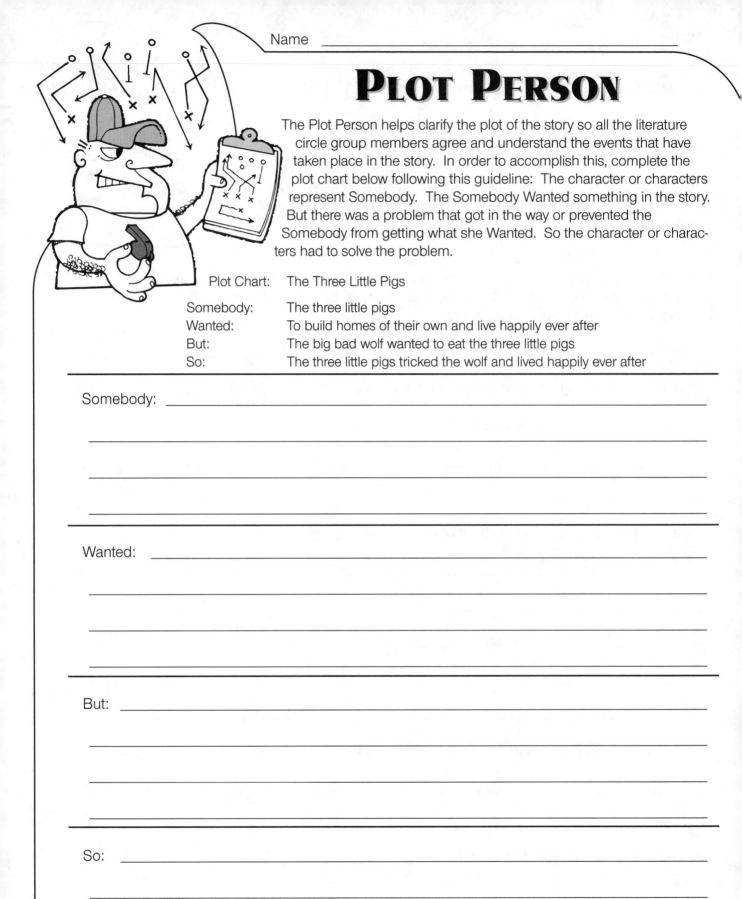

Name _____

PLOT PERSON

The Plot Person helps clarify the plot of the story so all the literature circle group members agree and understand the events that have taken place in the story. In order to accomplish this, complete the plot chart below following this guideline: The character or characters represent Somebody. The Somebody Wanted something in the story. But there was a problem that got in the way or prevented the Somebody from getting what she Wanted. So the character or characters had to solve the problem.

Plot Chart: The Three Little Pigs

Somebody: The three little pigs
Wanted: To build homes of their own and live happily ever after
But: The big bad wolf wanted to eat the three little pigs
So: The three little pigs tricked the wolf and lived happily ever after

Somebody: _____

_____

_____

_____

Wanted: _____

_____

_____

_____

But: _____

_____

_____

_____

So: _____

_____

_____

_____

32

HISTORY CONNECTOR

Your role as the History Connector is to provide your group members with accurate additional information about the historical events, places and people mentioned in your book. Historical fiction is based on actual historical events, and historical accuracy is important in this type of fiction even though the conversations of characters are usually fictitious.

As you read, use sticky notes to tag pages that mention historical events, places or people. After you've finished reading your assigned pages, go through your tagged pages and select four subjects for possible research and list them below. Gather general research materials and decide which subject you would like to read more about. Supply the requested information below and share it with your group when you meet for discussion.

The four subjects that I'm most interested in researching include:

_____   _____

_____   _____

Topic choice: _____

Title of first resource: _____

Title of second resource: _____

The reason I chose this topic and the reason this topic is significant in the story are because _____

_____

_____

_____

Historical facts and information about the topic: _____

_____

_____

_____

_____

_____

_____

_____

SCENE SETTER

The way an author describes a setting or an action can capture your imagination. Your role as the Scene Setter is to share your imagination with your group members by selecting three different scenes from the assigned reading and illustrating one in the space provided. After each scene, list three words that describe the scene.

Scene 1: _____ Page(s) _____

Three descriptive words: _____ _____ _____

Scene 2: _____ Page(s) _____

Three descriptive words: _____ _____ _____

Scene 3: _____ Page(s) _____

Three descriptive words: _____ _____ _____

I chose to illustrate the above scene because _____

_____

Culture-Customs Commentator

The beliefs and behaviors that are characteristic of a particular community or country make up that community's or country's culture. A custom is a part of a community's or country's culture because it is an established traditional practice that is followed by a group of people.

Many stories are set in various cultures which the author helps the reader understand by including examples of the culture's customs. For instance, in Scott O'Dell's *Sing Down the Moon*, the main character, Bright Morning, goes through a Womanhood Ceremony as required by her Native American culture. In a strikingly different culture, another custom related to growing up is required of Jonas as he attends his Ceremony of Twelve in Lois Lowry's *The Giver*.

Your role as the Culture-Customs Commentator is to help your group members explore and understand the culture described in your book and the instances where various customs are practiced.

This story takes place in the time period of _____

This story takes place in the country and community of _____

Besides naming the time period, country and community, the author gives the reader a sense of the time period and places by providing the reader with the following examples and clues: _____

_____

_____

Often clothing and transportation are examples of a country's and a community's culture. In this story, clothing and transportation are described as _____

_____

_____

Often authors use specific words and expressions which illustrate a country's or community's culture and customs. In this story, the following words and/or expressions are used: _____

_____

_____

Ceremonies are often examples of a country's or community's culture. In this story, the different ceremonies include: _____

_____

_____

_____

PASSAGE MASTER

Your role as the Passage Master is to help your group members zero in on special passages or important sections of the book. These passages are important because they may be sad, funny, dramatic, mysterious or descriptive in some way. The passages may be chunks of dialogue, a description of a house or one important sentence that adds to the story.

As you read, put sticky notes on the pages of passages you might want to bring to your group's attention. After you've finished reading your assigned pages, select the most important passages and provide the information below. **During your literature circle discussion, group members can take turns reading aloud the passages you've selected.**

Page(s) from which the passage is taken: _____

The passage begins with the following four words: _____

and ends with the following four words: _____

This passage is important because _____

_____

Page(s) from which the passage is taken: _____

The passage begins with the following four words: _____

and ends with the following four words: _____

This passage is important because _____

_____

Page(s) from which the passage is taken: _____

The passage begins with the following four words: _____

and ends with the following four words: _____

This passage is important because _____

_____

Page(s) from which the passage is taken: _____

The passage begins with the following four words: _____

and ends with the following four words: _____

This passage is important because _____

_____

Name _____

SEQUEL-PREQUEL PERSON

As the Sequel-Prequel Person, you have a choice of roles. First, you may wish to create a story that continues the story line after the ending of the original story. A story that continues an existing narration is called a sequel. On the other hand, you may wish to create a story that occurs before the opening of the original story. This type of story is called the prequel.

The questions below will help you organize the information you will need in order to write a sequel or prequel. Once you've carefully reviewed the information, write your sequel or prequel on a separate sheet of paper and read it aloud to your group members when you meet for discussion. During your literature circle discussion time, make sure to ask your group members to share their ideas for sequels and/or prequels.

A suggested title for my sequel is _____

As the present story continues, the following characters remain important: _____

_____

As the present story continues, the events of the story take place in the following location(s): _____

_____

As the present story continues, four significant events occur: _____

_____

The purpose of the new continuing story is to: _____

_____

A suggested title for my prequel is _____

The following characters are important in the prequel: _____

_____

In the story that occurs prior to the present story, the events of the story take place in the following

location(s): _____

_____

In the prequel story, the following four significant events occur prior to the events in the present story:

_____

_____

The purpose of the prequel story is _____

_____

Name _____

SCIENCE-GEOGRAPHY GENIUS

In many books science and geography are central elements in the story. For example, a nonfiction book about Admiral Byrd's expedition to Antarctica would require readers to understand weather-related science as well as the geographical difficulties of people living on Antarctica. At the same time, fiction books such as Jean Craighead George's *The Talking Earth* includes science as it relates to animals and ecosystems and includes such geographical terms as *bays, swamps, canals* and *sloughs*.

Your role as the Science-Geography Genius is to provide your group members with accurate additional information about the scientific and geographical elements mentioned in your book. As you read, use sticky notes to tag pages that mention scientific topics such as plants, animals, astronomy, weather systems and the environment. Also tag pages that mention geographical topics such as Earth formations, bodies of water, natural resources and conservation. Select four scientific and geographical topics for research and gather general research materials. After reviewing your materials, select one topic from each category and supply the additional information.

Possible Science-Related Topics

1. _____

2. _____

3. _____

4. _____

5. _____

Possible Geography-Related Topics

1. _____

2. _____

3. _____

4. _____

5. _____

Name _____

SCIENCE-GEOGRAPHY GENIUS

Selected Science Topic: _____

Research Resource: _____

Research Resource: _____

The science topic is important in the book because _____

_____

Additional information about science topic: _____

_____

_____

_____

_____

Selected Geography Topic: _____

Research Resource: _____

Research Resource: _____

The geography topic is important in the book because _____

_____

Additional information about geography topic: _____

_____

_____

_____

Name _____

STORY TREE TELLER

Your role as the Story Tree Teller is to help your group members focus on the basic literary elements of plot, character, setting, conflict, theme and mood. Use exact language to supply the required information for the Story Tree. During your group discussion, ask your group members to supply their own words to complete the Story Tree.

Write:
1. One word that describes the main character
2. Two words that describe the mood of the story
3. Three words that tell where the story takes place (setting)
4. Four words that tell the plot or main event of the story
5. Five words that describe the main conflict in the story
6. Six words that describe the message or theme of the story

DIALOGUE DESIGNER

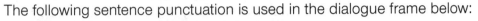

The role of the Dialogue Designer is to help group members put themselves into the action of the story by creating an imaginary conversation. This "dialogue" takes place between a character in the story and the Dialogue Designer and can be entertaining, persuasive or informative conversation.

The following sentence punctuation is used in the dialogue frame below:

The waitress said, "We bake all our own pies."
"We bake all our own pies," said the waitress.
"Because we bake all our own pies," said the waitress, "they're always fresh."
"We bake all our own pies," said the waitress. "They're guaranteed to be fresh."

Note: The boxes in the dialogue are for tag words such as *asked, shouted, exclaimed, whispered, said*, etc. The line with the * in front of it is where your character's name is written into the dialogue.

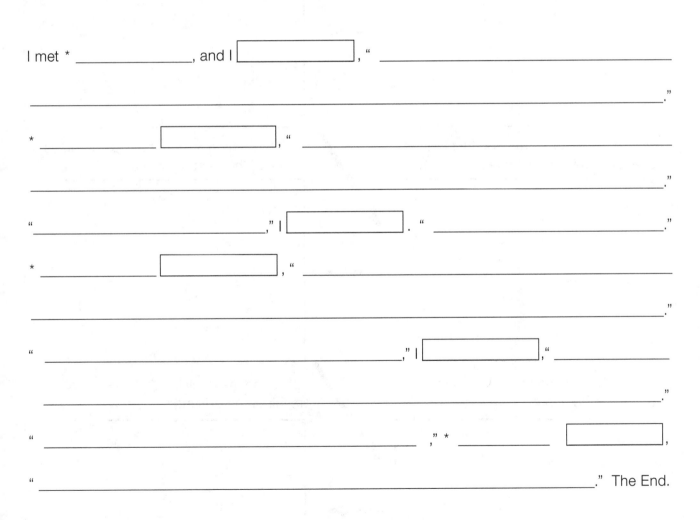

Name _____

DECISION DIRECTOR

In every fiction book, characters make decisions that move the story forward to its inevitable conclusion. In nonfiction books, people make decisions that impact the world around them. The role of the Decision Director is to help the group members look more closely at the decisions that are made in the book and how the decisions helped move the story forward to its conclusion. In the case of a nonfiction book, the Decision Director helps the group members look more closely at the decisions made by the people in the books and how those decisions impacted the world in positive and/or negative ways.

Describe the existing situation that led the character or person to make a decision.

Describe the decision that was made as a result of the existing situation.

Describe the existing situation that led the character or person to make a decision.

Describe the decision that was made as a result of the existing situation.

Describe the existing situation that led the character or person to make a decision.

Describe the decision that was made as a result of the existing situation.

Name _____

CONFLICT CONNECTOR

The literary element of conflict is the main struggle that takes place in the story. Most stories usually center around one of four basic types of conflict. The conflicts are:

      Character vs. Character
      Character vs. Nature
      Character vs. Himself or Herself
      Character vs. Laws or Customs of Society

Your role as the Conflict Connector is to help your group members understand the type of conflict that exists in your book and to discuss the various ways the character(s) works through the conflict in an attempt to resolve it.

In this story, does the main character struggle with another character? If so, give examples. _____

_____

_____

In this story, does the main character struggle with storms, hurricanes, forest fires or any other acts

of nature? If so, give examples: _____

_____

In this story does the main character struggle with himself or herself by being afraid, lonely, unhappy

or angry? If so, give examples: _____

_____

In this story, does the main character struggle with rules, laws or customs that he or she is expected

to obey? If so, give examples: _____

_____

Of the four different types of conflict or struggles listed above, which conflict was the most dominant

in the story? _____

_____

Identify three different ways the main character tried to resolve the conflict: _____

_____

_____

If you were the main character, would you have tried to resolve the conflict the same way or in a dif-

ferent way? Explain. _____

_____

SOLUTIONS SUGGESTER

In every story the main character encounters a problem or a series of problems and makes a number of decisions in order to arrive at successful solutions. Problem solving is a main ingredient of most storytelling.

Your role as the Solutions Suggester is to state clearly the main character's problem. In addition, it is your responsibility to list and evaluate the solutions that main character decides to use to solve the problem. Finally, it is your role to suggest alternative solutions the main character might have used to solve the problem and to explain how any alternative solution would change the story.

The most significant problem the main character encounters is _____

_____

The main character tries to solve the problem by _____

_____

In trying to solve his or her problem, the main character encounters some difficulties that include:

_____

_____

Two alternative solutions to the main character's problem are _____

_____ and

_____

If the main character had chosen the **first second** solution mentioned above, the story would
(Circle one.)

have changed because _____

_____

_____

In my opinion, the way the author resolved the main character's problems was _____

_____

_____

In addition to the main character's most significant problem, he or she encountered other problems

that included: _____

_____

These additional problems were solved when _____

_____

RECIPE READER

Your role as the Recipe Reader is to create a recipe that lists all the ingredients of your book, making it a book "good enough to eat." Your recipe ingredients include:

Plot: Tell the main events or happenings in the story.
Theme: Tell the message of the story. What is the author telling the reader?
Setting: Tell where the story takes place.
Mood: Tell if the story is funny, scarey, sad, exciting, mysterious, etc.
Character(s): Tell the names of the main characters and if they are helpful, mean, funny, honest, clever, friendly, etc.

During your group discussion, share your recipe with your group members. Let members include ingredients they feel add positively to the recipe.

Take one plot where _____

_____

_____

_____

Stir in _____

_____

_____

_____

Sprinkle with _____

_____

_____

_____

Top it all off with _____

_____

_____

_____

What do you get? _____

_____

Have-in-Common Connector

Your role as the Have-in-Common Connector is to help the group discover what they "have in common" with the characters, people and events in the fiction or nonfiction book. In addition, your role is to promote your group's discussion in order to discover how group members would react when faced by the same situations described in the book. Your final responsibility is to promote discussion to discover any connections between the book the group is currently reading and any other books members have read in the past. For your role, you will complete parts of this sheet **before** you meet for discussion and complete the rest of it **after** or **during** your discussion.

1. List ways in which you and any of your group members are similar to any of the characters or people

in the book. _____

_____

_____

2. Select two significant events from the book and summarize them below. During your discussion, ask what each of your group members would do if they were in the same situation.

    Event 1: _____

    Group decided they would _____

    Event 2: _____

    Group decided they would _____

3. Have you or anyone in your group been faced with the same types of situation as those described in

the book? If so, how did you and any of your group members respond? _____

_____

4. Is this book in any way similar to any other book you've read? Give titles and examples.

Title: _____   Author: _____

Examples: _____

_____

Title: _____   Author: _____

Examples: _____

_____

MAPMAKER

The Mapmaker creates a map or plots on an existing map the different places mentioned in the book and explains to the group any travel that takes place in the story. Use sticky notes to tag pages that contain the names of countries, states, provinces, cities, towns, streets, rivers, oceans, etc. After you've finished reading your assigned pages, go through your tagged pages and select 10 places that are important to the story or nonfiction book. Spell correctly and note pages.

1. _____, pages _____   6. _____, pages _____

2. _____, pages _____   7. _____, pages _____

3. _____, pages _____   8. _____, pages _____

4. _____, pages _____   9. _____, pages _____

5. _____, pages _____   10. _____, pages _____

If the characters or people in the book traveled between cities, countries, etc., list the travel and the distance below.

Name of character(s)/person _____ traveled from _____

to _____. He/She/They traveled _____ miles (km).

Describe any additional travel that involved other characters. _____

_____

Explain the significance of the travel that took place in the book. _____

_____

_____

Do one of the following:
- Draw a small map on the back of this sheet noting the 10 items listed above.
- On an existing map, highlight the 10 items listed above.

PROGRESS-PROCESS PERSON

The role of the Progress-Process Person is to assess the process and progress of the literature circle group and its discussion. Your evaluation **will not** be used when determining group members' grades. Instead, the assessment sheet below should give a "snapshot" of how your group did in terms of discussing the book and working cooperatively.

Progress

Title of book: _____ Author: _____

Date of literature circle discussion: _____ Pages discussed: _____

The most important thing we talked about in today's discussion was _____

_____

Our plans for our next group discussion are _____

_____

Process: A = Always   O = Often   S = Sometimes   N = Never   Y = Yes   NN = No

Name: _____   Role: _____

_____   Came to the discussion completely prepared (pages read and role sheet done).

_____   Contributed to the group's discussion yet encouraged others to contribute also.

_____   Remained focused on the discussion (no distracting/inappropriate behavior).

Name: _____   Role: _____

_____   Came to the discussion completely prepared (pages read and role sheet done).

_____   Contributed to the group's discussion yet encouraged others to contribute also.

_____   Remained focused on the discussion (no distracting/inappropriate behavior).

Name: _____   Role: _____

_____   Came to the discussion completely prepared (pages read and role sheet done).

_____   Contributed to the group's discussion yet encouraged others to contribute also.

_____   Remained focused on the discussion (no distracting/inappropriate behavior).

Name: _____   Role: _____

_____   Came to the discussion completely prepared (pages read and role sheet done).

_____   Contributed to the group's discussion yet encouraged others to contribute also.

_____   Remained focused on the discussion (no distracting/inappropriate behavior).

The best/worst thing that happened in our discussion today was _____

_____

Name _____

TIME LINER

Your role as the Time Liner is to create a time line that chronicles the important events in your fiction or nonfiction book.

As you read your assigned pages, use sticky notes to tag pages of events you think may be important enough to record on your time line. After you've finished reading, select 10 events and record them in the proper sequence below. Some important events might be the introduction of a new character, a battle, a natural disaster, a character's accomplishments, a move, a journey, a birth or a death. During your literature circle discussion, you will need to explain why you chose the events to include on your time line and allow group members to add additional important events if they wish.

1. _____

     Page(s) _____

2. _____

     Page(s) _____

3. _____

     Page(s) _____

4. _____

     Page(s) _____

5. _____

     Page(s) _____

6. _____

     Page(s) _____

7. _____

     Page(s) _____

8. _____

     Page(s) _____

9. _____

     Page(s) _____

10. _____

     Page(s) _____

Tangrams Teller

Tangrams are ancient Chinese puzzles. Storytellers use the puzzle pieces, called tans, when they tell stories. Your role as the Tangrams Teller is to cut out the puzzle pieces below and use them during discussion to retell a brief portion of the story.

1. Select the portion of the story you plan to retell. (You should plan to rearrange the tans at least three times during your storytelling.)

2. Cut out the tans below and rearrange them to represent different characters, scenes or objects from the story.

3. Practice telling the story and arranging the tans.

QUOTABLE QUOTATIONS QUIZZER

Famous people are often remembered for the words they said or wrote. At the same time, story characters are often remembered for their words. These "quotable quotations" can range from Abraham Lincoln's words, "Four score and seven years ago . . ." from the *Gettysburg Address* to Dorothy's famous words, "There's no place like home" from *The Wizard of Oz*.

Your role as the Quotable Quotations Quizzer is to help your group members recognize important statements made by famous people or characters in your book and discuss each quotation's significance. During group discussion, you can "quiz" your group members by reading each quotation aloud and asking members to guess who said it and explain why he or she guessed that person or character.

Quotation: _____

_____

Quotation said by _____ Page(s) _____

This quotation is important because _____

Quotation: _____

_____

Quotation said by _____ Page(s) _____

This quotation is important because _____

Quotation: _____

_____

Quotation said by _____ Page(s) _____

This quotation is important because _____

Quotation: _____

_____

Quotation said by _____ Page(s) _____

This quotation is important because _____

Name _____

QUOTABLE QUOTATIONS QUIZZER

Quotation: _____

_____

Quotation said by _____ Page(s) _____

This quotation is important because _____

_____

Quotation: _____

_____

Quotation said by _____ Page(s) _____

This quotation is important because _____

_____

Quotation: _____

_____

Quotation said by _____ Page(s) _____

This quotation is important because _____

_____

Quotation: _____

_____

Quotation said by _____ Page(s) _____

This quotation is important because _____

_____

Quotation: _____

_____

Quotation said by _____ Page(s) _____

This quotation is important because _____

MATH MAGICIAN

Nonfiction books often contain statistics that can be used to create math problems. Answering these math problems can often help readers interpret and put into perspective the statistics they read in their books. For example, the following is a statement from Jim Murphy's *The Great Fire*. See how the information from the statement is used to create a math problem and how the answer to the math problem is related to the book.

Statistics: "In 1863 there had been 186 reported fires in Chicago; the number had risen to 515 by 1868. Records for 1870 indicate that fire-fighting companies responded to nearly 600 alarms." (p. 19)

Math Problem: Create a bar graph that illustrates the increase in the number of fires from 1863 to 1870. Next, tell what percentage this increase represents.

Significance: The fact that Chicago had over a 200 percent increase in fires from 1863 to 1870 indicates that Chicago was a growing city, and its potential for fires was growing as well. The book states, by 1871 Chicago "was a city ready to burn." (p. 18)

Your role as Math Magician is to select interesting statistics from your book and use those statistics to create math problems for your group to solve and to relate the significance of your math problem answer to the book. Although it will be your responsibility to create and complete your math problem before the group meets for discussion, during discussion group members should work together to solve the math problems. In addition, members can add their own ideas as to the significance of the math problem answer and its relationship to the book.

Statistics: _____

_____ (p.   )

Math Problem: _____

_____

Significance: _____

Statistics: _____

_____ (p.   )

Math Problem: _____

_____

Significance: _____

Name _____

MATH MAGICIAN

Statistics: _____

_____ (p.   )

Math Problem: _____

_____

Significance: _____

Statistics: _____

_____ (p.   )

Math Problem: _____

_____

Significance: _____

Statistics: _____

_____ (p.   )

Math Problem: _____

_____

Significance: _____

Statistics: _____

_____ (p.   )

Math Problem: _____

_____

Significance: _____

WORDSMITH

Your role as Wordsmith is to help introduce new, interesting and important words to your literature group members. As you read, use sticky notes to tag pages where you find words you'd like to share with your group. During your discussion time, have students take turns reading the sentences aloud and discussing possible meanings of words. Make sure you explain what the word means as it is used in the sentence and write an original sentence, using the word correctly.

Word: _____ Part of Speech: _____ Page: _____

Definition of the word as it's used in the sentence: _____

Original sentence: _____

_____

Word: _____ Part of Speech: _____ Page: _____

Definition of the word as it's used in the sentence: _____

Original sentence: _____

_____

Word: _____ Part of Speech: _____ Page: _____

Definition of the word as it's used in the sentence: _____

Original sentence: _____

_____

Word: _____ Part of Speech: _____ Page: _____

Definition of the word as it's used in the sentence: _____

Original sentence: _____

_____

WORDSMITH

Word: _____ Part of Speech: _____ Page: _____

Definition of the word as it's used in the sentence: _____

Original sentence: _____

_____

Word: _____ Part of Speech: _____ Page; _____

Definition of the word as it's used in the sentence: _____

Original sentence: _____

_____

Word: _____ Part of Speech: _____ Page: _____

Definition of the word as it's used in the sentence: _____

Original sentence: _____

_____

Word: _____ Part of Speech: _____ Page: _____

Definition of the word as it's used in the sentence: _____

Original sentence: _____

_____

Word: _____ Part of Speech: _____ Page: _____

Definition of the word as it's used in the sentence: _____

Original sentence: _____

_____

Name _____

Classroom Library
Inventory Sheet

Title	Author	Number of Books

Name _____

CLASSROOM LIBRARY
INVENTORY SHEET

Title   Author   Number of Books

_____

_____

_____

_____

_____

_____

_____

_____

_____

_____

_____

_____

_____

_____

_____

_____

_____

_____

Name _____

AUTHOR-BASED LITERATURE CIRCLE INVENTORY SHEET

Author: _____

Titles   Number of Books

_____

_____

_____

_____

Author: _____

Titles   Number of Books

_____

_____

_____

_____

Author: _____

Titles   Number of Books

_____

_____

_____

_____

Name _____

AUTHOR-BASED LITERATURE CIRCLE
INVENTORY SHEET

Author: _____

Titles   Number of Books

_____

_____

_____

_____

Author: _____

Titles   Number of Books

_____

_____

_____

_____

Author: _____

Titles   Number of Books

_____

_____

_____

_____

Name _____

Genre-Based Literature Circle Inventory Sheet

Genre: _____

Title   Author   Number of Books

_____

_____

_____

_____

Genre: _____

Title   Author   Number of Books

_____

_____

_____

_____

Genre: _____

Title   Author   Number of Books

_____

_____

_____

_____

Name _____

Genre-Based Literature Circle Inventory Sheet

Genre: _____

Title   Author   Number of Books

_____

_____

_____

_____

Genre: _____

Title   Author   Number of Books

_____

_____

_____

_____

Genre: _____

Title   Author   Number of Books

_____

_____

_____

_____

Name _____

Theme-Based Literature Circle Inventory Sheet

Theme: _____

Title   Author   Number of Books

_____

_____

_____

_____

Theme: _____

Title   Author   Number of Books

_____

_____

_____

_____

Theme: _____

Title   Author   Number of Books

_____

_____

_____

_____

Name _____

THEME-BASED LITERATURE CIRCLE
INVENTORY SHEET

Theme: _____

Title   Author   Number of Books

_____

_____

_____

_____

Theme: _____

Title   Author   Number of Books

_____

_____

_____

_____

Theme: _____

Title   Author   Number of Books

_____

_____

_____

_____